CAT-a-PULT
A LITTLE GUIDE

RP Minis®
Hachette Book Group
1290 Avenue of the Americas, New York, NY 10104
www.runningpress.com
@Running_Press

First Edition: October 2021

Published by RP Minis, an imprint of Perseus Books, LLC, a subsidiary of Hachette Book Group, Inc. The RP Minis name and logo is a registered trademark of the Hachette Book Group.

ISBN: 978-0-7624-7372-4

CONTENTS

INTRODUCTION

Welcome to Cat-a-Pult—the only game that's more fun than trying to catch a laser pointer. It's like catnip for game lovers!

If you thought acrobats on trapezes were the pinnacle of aerial sports, picture this: Three cats, donning flowing capes, climbing eagerly into a welcoming, oversized cat paw. The paw's arm is tugged slowly back, back, back, until you have that superb tension—and SNAP! The superstars rocket upward in a glorious airborne arc onto the comfort of a landing mat filled with tasty treats.

This game was made especially for all of those ailurophiles ("cat lovers" in layman's terms) out there. Statistically speaking, you're one of them! And why wouldn't you be? Cats are the epitome of cool—there's literally the term "cool cat." Cats do everything on their own terms and can jump up into the air up to five times their own height. How far they can fly from a cat-a-pult, of course, is up to you!

FOR THE LOVE OF CATS

Did you know cats are the most popular pet in the US? There are approximately 94 million pet cats living in the States, which is about four million more than the number of pet dogs. Sorry, Rover, but *felis catus* rules this roost.

Cats of all types have nuzzled into a special place in people's hearts through the years. Here's a lil' round-up of some of the most famous cats around:

FELIX THE CAT

Despite getting his start in the silent film era, Felix the Cat might have one of the most recognizable theme songs among his feline friends. Famous for his magical bag of tricks, Felix shows up as an icon and mascot in a wide variety of American pop culture.

SYLVESTER

Sufferin' succotash! Sylvester is always chasing that pesky Tweety Bird to no avail, but you have to admire that he never gives up. He should be proud of himself, though—Sylvester has the most Academy Awards® of any Looney Tunes character, with three Oscars® earned for films he starred in.

CHESHIRE CAT

The oldest of the kitties on this list, the Cheshire Cat made his debut in the novel *Alice's Adventures in Wonderland* by

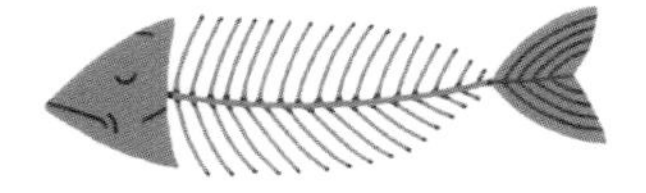

Lewis Carroll, published all the way back in 1865. The Cheshire Cat's iconic grin, which sometimes is the only visible part of his body, somehow both pleases and perturbs the imagination.

GARFIELD

Leaning hard into cats' reputation as lazy, Garfield's sole delights in life seem to be naps, loathing Mondays, and lasagna. Fun fact: Garfield's creator, Jim Davis, grew up on a farm with twenty-five cats.

GRUMPY CAT

This charming cat, with a permanently grumpy face, made her debut in 2012 and is probably the most famous of the internet celebrity cats. Despite her sad and untimely passing in 2019, she remains the subject of thousands of memes. Fun fact: Grumpy Cat actually had dwarfism and an underbite, which gave her the unique appearance millions adored.

ALL OF THE CATS IN *CATS*, THE MUSICAL

T.S. Eliot had a rush of feline inspiration once and wrote a poetry book about "practical cats;" remarkably—over forty years later—the poems were transformed into a full-length play starring dozens of anthropomorphized cats singing songs. With names like Grizabella, Rum Tum Tugger, and Rumpleteazer, *Cats* continues to be a wacky worldwide sensation that's still amusing audiences of all kinds.

PLAYING THE GAME

Find yourself a fur-midable opponent and play the cat-a-pult game!

SETUP

Inside this kit you'll find:

- A cat-a-pult, in the form of a colossal cat paw
- 3 flying cats, donning daredevil capes
- A landing mat, featuring all of our kitty crusaders' favorite things

Position the landing mat a few feet from the cat-a-pult. You can determine if you're playing a tabby's length or a tiger's length away, depending on if you're feeling laying-around-the-house lethargic or pouncing-on-a-bird peppy. Pop open a fresh can of tuna or grab some kibble, and get ready to caterwaul in excitement.

HOW TO PLAY

Whichever player has lived the most lives, or is longest in the whiskers, goes first. Each player takes a turn flinging three cats. The first player should place their first cat in the cat-a-pult and pull the big paw backward slightly—releasing the tension when the cat-a-pult is taut—and launch their kitty onto the mat. After discharging all three cats, the first player should then

3
5
10
5
3

count up their points, depending on where the cats land on the mat:

CENTER RING: 10 points

MIDDLE RING: 5 points

OUTER RING: 3 points

EDGE OF THE MAT: 0 points

OFF THE MAT: 0 points
(but you can take another turn)

The next player should take their turn and count up their points and so on. After everyone has taken a turn, evaluate how everyone did:

0 POINTS:

Sorry, you used up all of your nine lives. Every kitty deserves multiple chances, but you really pushed that to the limit, huh? Sharpen your claws on the scratching post and prepare to redeem yourself next time.

3 POINTS:

Like a black cat crossing your path, you're a bit unlucky. Maybe you coughed up a hairball and it got in the way of your flinging skills. Lick your wounds and try again.

5–9 POINTS:

True feline indifference. You're not looking to be the cat who catches the most mice, but you're not about to vie for the Laziest Cat award, either. It's better than a dog would do, anyway.

10–14 POINTS:

A real hep cat. Twirl your whiskers in celebration—you've got a real knack for this thing! You must have quite the pedigree.

15+ POINTS:

The real cat's meow. Lap it up! You're a true winner. Go curl up with a nice warm laptop and congratulate yourself.

At the end of the game, the player with the most points wins the game. Loser has to scratch the winner behind the ears.

CAT FACTS, JOKES, AND LORE

There is an abundance of fascinating facts and intriguing information about cats. Enjoy swapping these facts, jokes, and lore while you're hurling those plucky pussy-cats across the room.

Cats' kidneys can filter out salt, which means that in a pinch they could drink seawater to hydrate.

The scientific name for a hairball is *bezoar*.

Cats have balance organs in their inner ears to help them right themselves in mid-air and land on their feet.

House cats share 95.6 percent of their genetic makeup with tigers.

"Sense of humor" might not be the *first* thing that comes to mind when thinking of our feline friends, but that doesn't mean you can't giggle at a few puns and quips about 'em.

Q: Why was the cat afraid of the tree?

A: Because of its bark

Q: What do you call a cat who loves to bowl?

A: An alley cat

A cat walks into a bar.
The bartender says, "What'll you have?"
The cat says, "A shot of whiskey."
The bartender pours the cat his drink.
Slowly, the cat pushes the shot off the
bar until it spills and crashes.
"Another," demands the cat.

Cats have not only inspired humans to chase a feather on a string for hours, but they've also inspired science, archaeology, politics, and linguistics. Read on to learn some alluring lore.

Inventor Nikola Tesla was inspired to experiment with electricity after his cat gave him a static-electric shock.

For one of his early films in 1894, inventor Thomas Edison filmed two cats "boxing" inside a little ring.

Félicette, also known as Astrocat, was the first and only cat to go to space in 1963.

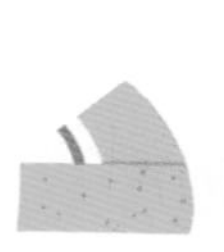

The Hungarian word for "quotation marks," *macskaköröm*, literally translates to "cat claws."

Egyptians are often given credit for domesticating cats, but the oldest known pet cat was discovered in a 9,500-year-old cat grave in Cyprus.

Hopefully you've now enjoyed a little playful time with your cat-a-pult and are now an expert in how to propel stunt-kitties into orbit. Or at least a few feet in front of you.

Now go enjoy some well-deserved cuddle time with your favorite loving and loyal cat. It'll be purrfect.

This book has been bound using handcraft methods and Smyth-sewn to ensure durability.

Designed by Jenna McBride.

Illustrated by Montse Galbany.

Written by Sarah Royal.